MUSICAL FANTASIES

7 Enchanting Late Elementary to Early Intermediate Piano Solos

June C. Montgomery

Welcome to a magical musical fantasy land—a land of enchanted forests, sprites and dragons! From *Sprites at Play* to *Dreadful Dragons*, these pieces are designed to express the many different styles and moods that are found in this entrancing world.

I hope that as you play these pieces you will enjoy a great adventure in this whimsical land of musical fantasy!

June C. Montgomery

ISBN 0-7390-1885-X

Alfred

for Kate

SPRITES AT PLAY

June C. Montgomery

17
p
mp
21
mf
rit.
25
a tempo
8va
mp
29
mf
8va
f

for Anne

BEWITCHING BOOGIE

June C. Montgomery

17
mp
21
mf
25
f
mp
29
mf
f
mp
RH

for David

DREADFUL DRAGON

June C. Montgomery

17
21
25
mf
29
Slower
f
ff

for Hannah

MAGIC WAND

June C. Montgomery

13
8va
RH
mf
LH
mp
rit. poco a poco
16
a tempo
8va
RH
RH
mf
p
LH
LH
19
8va
RH
RH
mp
p
RH
LH
LH
mf
p
22
RH
8va
RH
LH
LH
RH
LH
mp
8va
rit.
f

for my grandchildren

DEEP, MYSTERIOUS POOL

June C. Montgomery

Slowly, with a clear, bell-like tone (𝅗𝅥 = 56)

Play both hands one octave lower than written

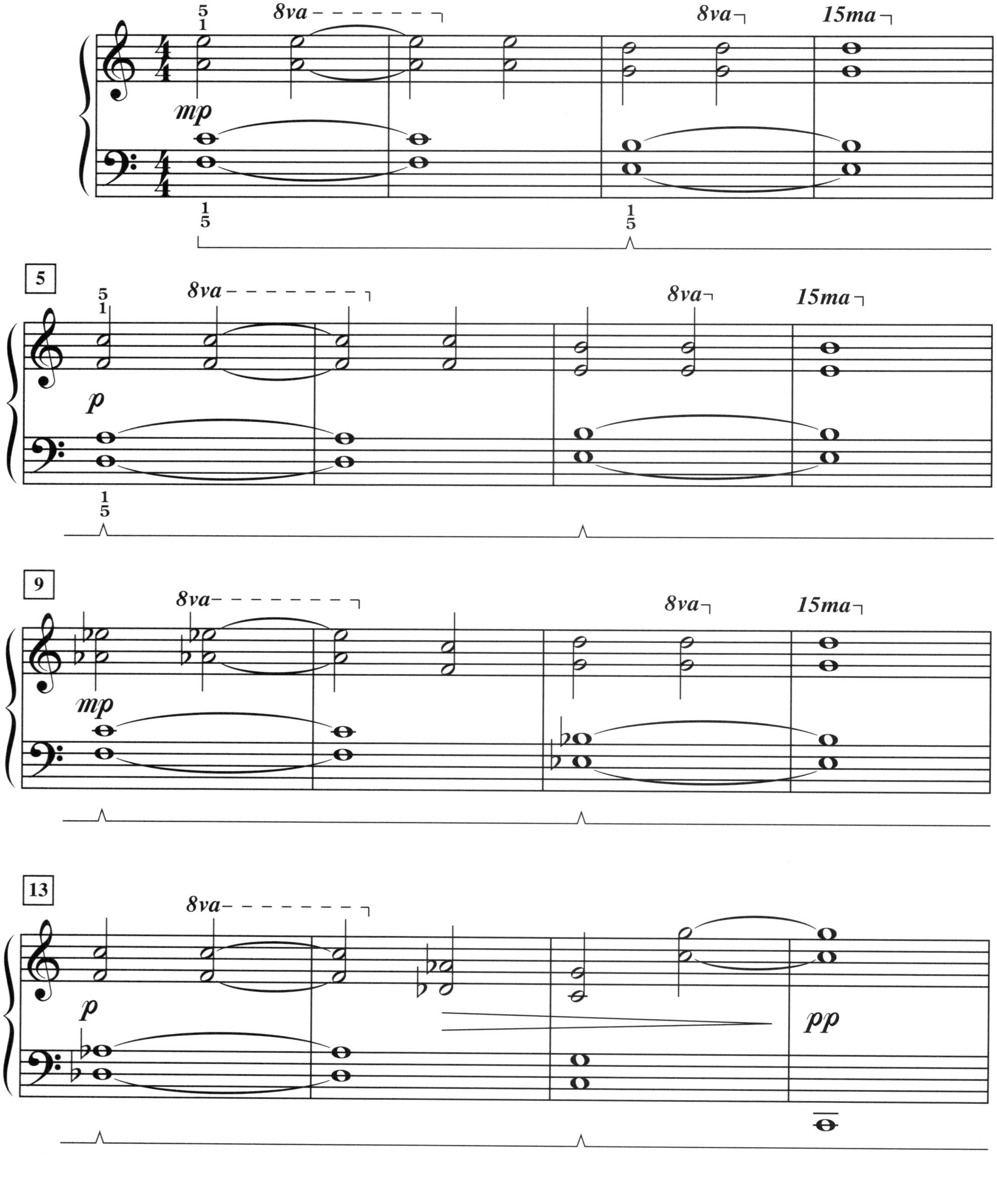

Play both hands as written
mp
p
8va
rit.
mf
a tempo
15ma
molto rit.
pp

for Mary Beth

SECRET, MOONLIT GARDEN

June C. Montgomery

17
21
rit.
a tempo
25
29
rit.
33
a tempo
Both hands 8va
loco

for Emily

ENCHANTED FOREST

June C. Montgomery

Mysteriously (♩ = 96)

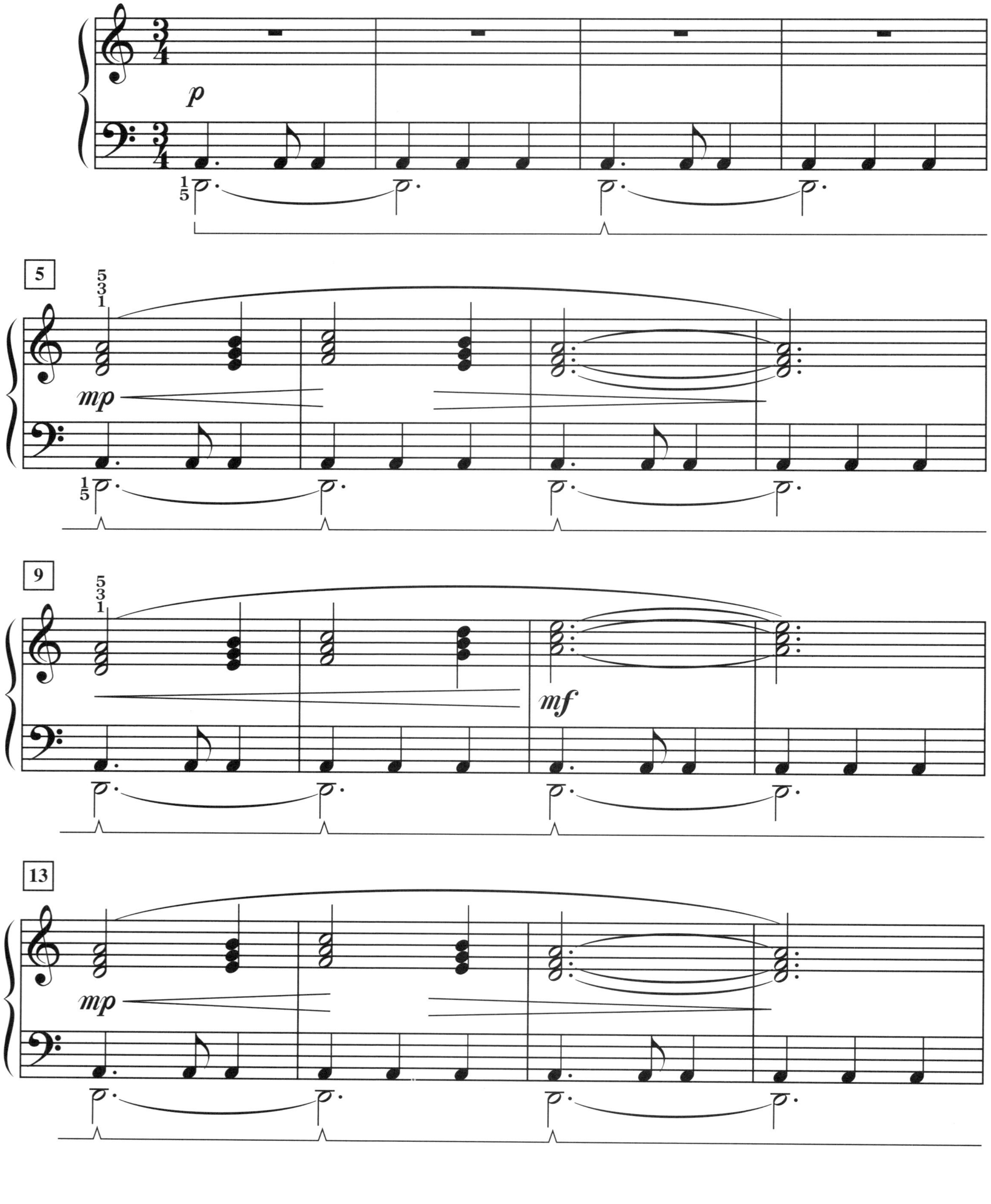

17
p
rit.
21
A little faster (♩ = 116)
mf
p
25
29
p
mf

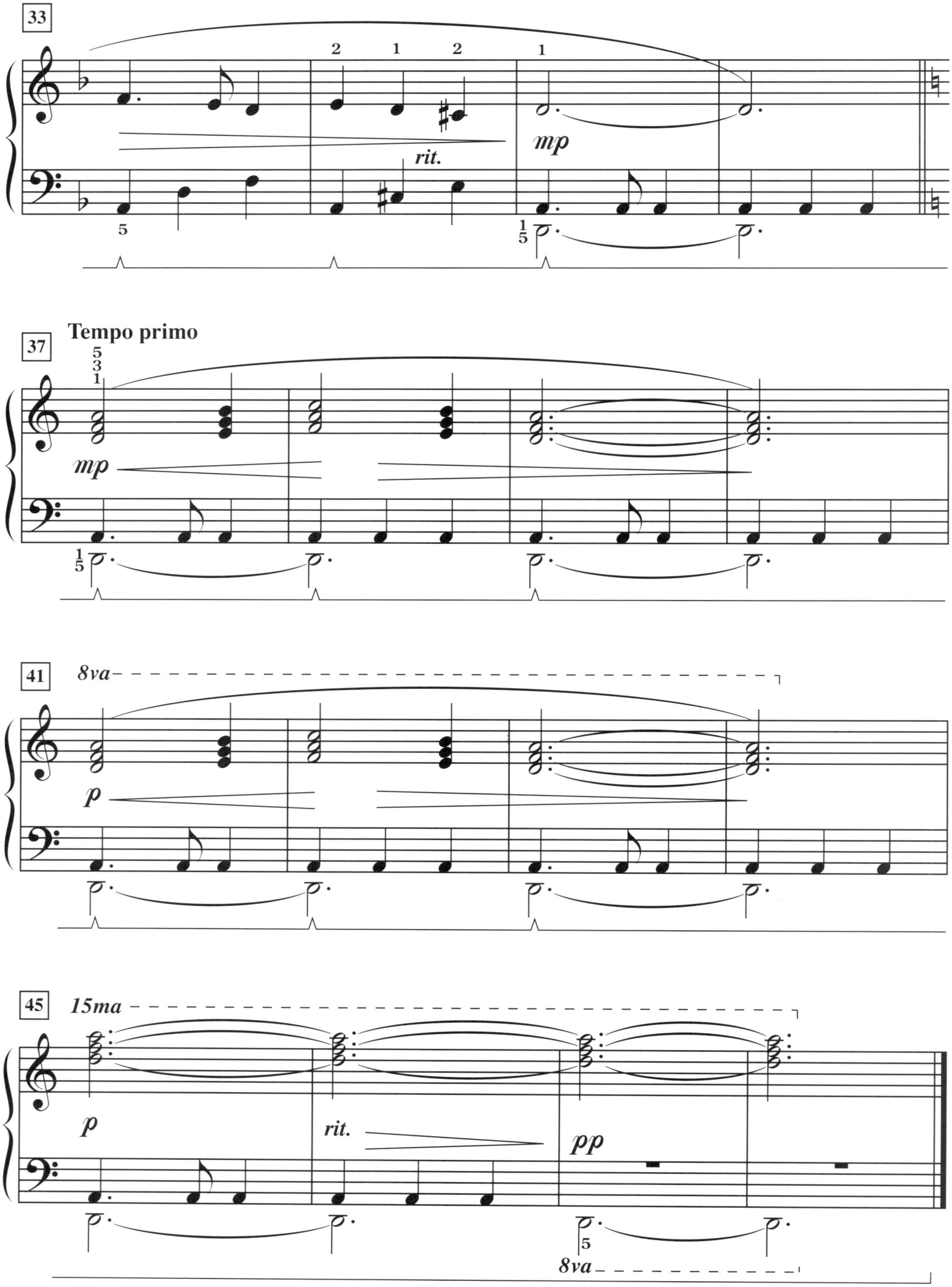
33
rit.
mp
37
Tempo primo
mp
41
8va
p
45
15ma
p
rit.
pp
8va